Countries Around the World

Liberia

Robin S. Doak

www.raintreepublishers.co.uk
Visit our website to find out more information about Raintree books.

To order:
☎ Phone 0845 6044371
🖷 Fax +44 (0) 1865 312263
🖳 Email myorders@raintreepublishers.co.uk

Customers from outside the UK please telephone +44 1865 312262

Raintree is an imprint of Capstone Global Library Limited, a company incorporated in England and Wales having its registered office at 7 Pilgrim Street, London, EC4V 6LB – Registered company number: 6695582

Edited by Abby Colich and Megan Cotugno
Designed by Philippa Jenkins
Original illustrations © Capstone Global Library Ltd.
Illustrated by Oxford Designers & Illustrators
Picture research by Liz Alexander
Originated by Capstone Global Library Ltd.
Printed in China by CTPS

ISBN 978 1 406 23563 0 (hardback)
16 15 14 13 12
10 9 8 7 6 5 4 3 2 1

British Library Cataloguing in Publication Data
Doak, Robin S. (Robin Santos), 1963-
  Liberia. -- (Countries around the world)
  1. Liberia--Juvenile literature.
  I. Title II. Series
  966.6'2033-dc22

Acknowledgements
We would like to thank the following for permission to reproduce photographs:Alamy: pp. 5 (© JS Callahan/tropicalpix), 21 (© Aurora Photos), 31 (© Simon Reddy), 39 (© Richard Smith); © CORBIS: p. 7; Corbis: pp. 15 (© Eldad Rafaeli), 32 (© Werner Forman), 36 (© Albrecht G. Schaefer); Dreamstime.com: p. 18 (© Nsonic); Getty Images: pp. 9 (Pascal Guyot/AFP), 10 (Michael Nagle), 11 (Issouf Sanogo/AFP), 24 (RAVEENDRAN/AFP), 25 (Glenna Gordon/AFP), 33 (Simon Bruty/Sports Illustrated), 34 (Glenna Gordon); Photolibrary: pp. 17 (Peter Arnold Images), 19 (Gilles Nicolet), 23 (Jacques Jangoux), 27 (Ron Giling), 29 (Edgar Cleijne), 30 (Ron Giling), 35 (Eye Ubiquitous); Shutterstock: p. 46 (© Kurt De Bruyn).

Cover photograph of women fishing with hand nets in shallow stream, West Africa, Liberia, Kpelle tribe, reproduced with permission from Photolibrary (Jacques Jangoux).

We would like to thank Shiera S. el-Malik for her invaluable help in the preparation of this book.

Every effort has been made to contact copyright holders of material reproduced in this book. Any omissions will be rectified in subsequent printings if notice is given to the publisher.

Contents

Some words are printed in bold, **like this**. You can find out what they mean by looking in the glossary.

Introducing Liberia

What do you know about the small African country of Liberia? If you've heard about Liberia's unusual history, you might know that some of the country's founders were freed American slaves. If you follow the news, you might know that Liberia is recovering from years of **civil war** and violence. If you love nature, you might know that Liberia is home to most of the remaining tropical rainforests in West Africa.

Liberia is all of these things, and much more. Located just north of the **equator**, this hot, **humid** nation is famed for its wild beauty. Rare and **endangered** animals make their homes in the country's forests. Breathtaking mountains, waterfalls, and beaches may one day attract people from around the world.

The country's written history may be short compared with other world nations, but it is unique. Unlike other parts of Africa, Liberia was never **colonized** by European explorers. It is also the oldest **republic** in Africa. And it was the first African nation to elect a female leader.

Liberia is known for its friendly, open people. But in the recent past, these people have faced the horrors of 14 years of civil war. Thousands of Liberians were killed, and hundreds of thousands fled the country. Now, Liberians are working together to overcome their difficult past and create a better future.

Liberia's landscape ranges from beaches and swamps to mountains and tropical rainforests.

History: a free nation of former slaves

The first people to settle in what is now Liberia migrated from other parts of Africa in the 1100s. These early arrivals were the ancestors of the Bassa, Dey, Gola, Kissi, and Kru people who still live in Liberia today. By the early 1800s, 16 different **tribes** had made their homes in Liberia.

During the 1500s and 1600s, most of Africa fell under European rule. Explorers from Britain, France, Portugal, and other nations claimed huge sections of land. The only part of Africa to remain unconquered was Liberia. It is the only African country never to have been a European **colony**.

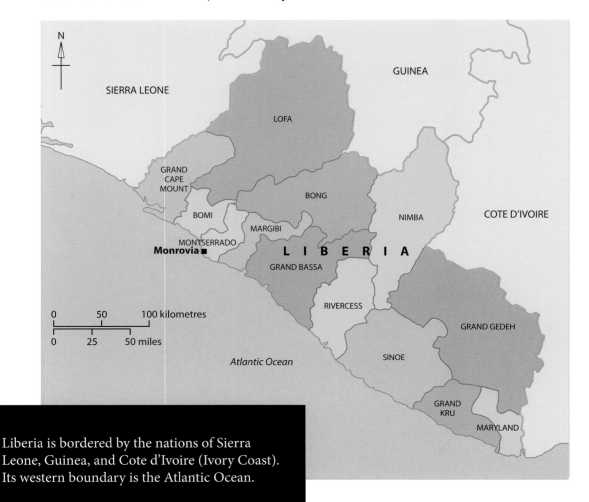

Liberia is bordered by the nations of Sierra Leone, Guinea, and Cote d'Ivoire (Ivory Coast). Its western boundary is the Atlantic Ocean.

Members of the Liberian Senate of 1893, shown here, were mostly freed African American slaves.

A refuge for freed slaves

In 1822 freed slaves from the United States began arriving in Liberia with the help of the American Colonization Society. This organization, made up of both **abolitionists** and slave owners, raised money to send free blacks to Africa. The group also **negotiated** with tribal leaders in the area to buy land.

Society members named the new colony Liberia, for liberty and freedom. The first town was called Monrovia in honour of US president James Monroe. Monroe supported the society's work.

Africa's first republic

Over the next 25 years, freed blacks continued to leave the United States for Liberia. These people became known as **Americo-Liberians**. In 1847 they declared their independence and formed their own government, a **republic**. Liberia was Africa's first republic.

Growing problems

From the time they arrived, the Americo-Liberians made up just a very small portion of Liberia's population. But this tiny group of people controlled the nation's power and wealth. From 1847 to 1980, they were in charge of Liberia's government. This caused anger and resentment within the native tribes in Liberia.

The new arrivals tried to **convert** the tribes in Liberia to Christianity. Tribes did not want to give up their religions, and this caused even more problems. Violent battles occurred occasionally between the native people and the Americo-Liberians.

Civil war

In 1989, the problems that had been simmering for more than 100 years erupted into a bloody **civil war**. Over the next seven years, several different groups warred against one another in hopes of controlling the government. The war ended in 1996, and elections for president were held the following year. In all, one out of every 17 Liberians died during the conflict.

YOUNG PEOPLE

During Liberia's first civil war, thousands of boys and girls were kidnapped from their families. Children as young as eight years old were given guns. They were forced to fight and kill others. After the war ended, groups like the **United Nations** Children's Fund (UNICEF) worked to help child soldiers fit back into normal life. They helped many find their families and return to school or get jobs. Today, efforts continue to help these former fighters give up violence and live peacefully.

Fighting during Liberia's first civil war caused the deaths of up to 250,000 people and forced a million more to flee to **refugee** camps in nearby countries.

A second civil war

In 1999, a second civil war began in Liberia. **Rebel** forces in the northern part of the country began killing people and destroying homes and property. The rebels wanted to overthrow Liberian president Charles Taylor. By 2002 about 230,000 Liberians had fled to other countries to escape the violence.

ELLEN JOHNSON SIRLEAF (B.1938)

In 2005, Liberians elected Ellen Johnson Sirleaf as their president. Sirleaf was the first female ever elected to serve as leader of an African country. Born in Monrovia in 1938, Sirleaf is an expert in **economics** and banking. In 1985 she was sentenced to 10 years in prison for speaking out against Liberia's **corrupt** president, Samuel Doe. During her first term as president, Sirleaf worked to help her nation recover from its two devastating civil wars. She has the support of many leaders around the world. Sirleaf was reelected in 2010.

Liberian women protest against violence outside peace talks held in Ghana.

Women for peace

In 2003, thousands of women banded together and formed the Women of Liberia Mass Action for Peace. Their goal was to end the violence throughout their country. In June many of the women travelled to Ghana to stand watch at peace talks there. They held **non-violent protests** and forced rival Liberian leaders to negotiate a **peace treaty**.

In August all sides agreed to end the war. They also agreed to hold elections for the next president. The United Nations (UN) sent in peacekeeping troops to make sure the treaty was followed. The UN also offered rebels money and job training if they turned in their weapons.

Regions and resources: the land of Liberia

Liberia is situated just north of the **equator**. As a result, the climate is hot all year round, with temperatures that climb regularly to 27° or 32°C (80° or 90°F). The country is also very **humid**, especially along the coast.

There are two major seasons in Liberia. The dry season runs from May to October. The rainy season is from November to April. During the dry season, winds called *harmattan* blow from the Sahara Desert across the land. Clean drinking water can become scarce in some areas during the dry season.

Regions

Liberia may be small in size, but its landscape is very varied. The coastal region is made up of low plains. Swamps, lagoons, and sand bars are all found in this area. The coast is the rainiest, most humid region of the country.

Away from the coast are plateaus covered with thick tropical forests. In the country's northern region there are low mountain ranges. Many rivers run across Liberia, stretching from the mountains to the ocean.

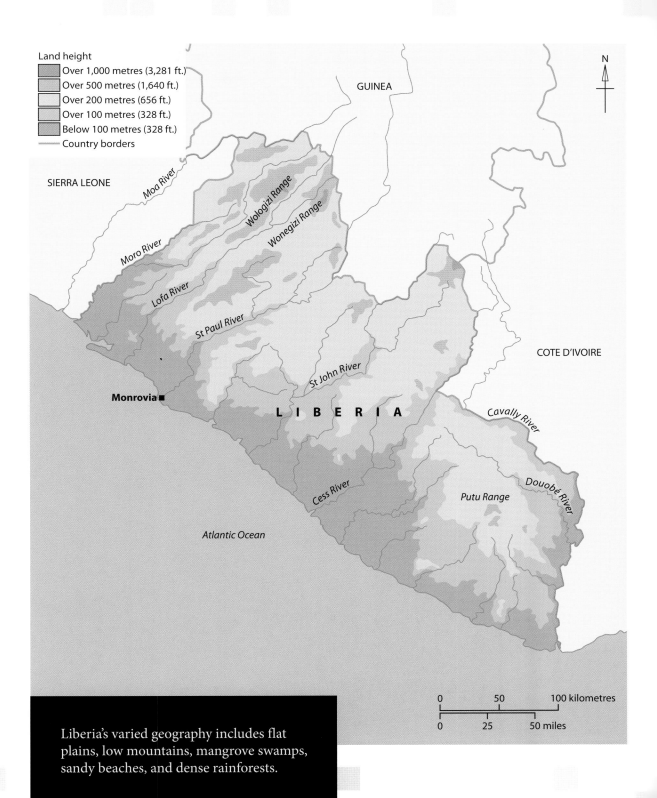

Land height
Over 1,000 metres (3,281 ft.)
Over 500 metres (1,640 ft.)
Over 200 metres (656 ft.)
Over 100 metres (328 ft.)
Below 100 metres (328 ft.)
—— Country borders

GUINEA

SIERRA LEONE

Moa River

Wologizi Range

Wonegizi Range

Moro River

Lofa River

St Paul River

St John River

COTE D'IVOIRE

Monrovia ■

L I B E R I A

Cavally River

Douobé River

Cess River

Putu Range

Atlantic Ocean

N

0   50   100 kilometres

0   25   50 miles

Liberia's varied geography includes flat
plains, low mountains, mangrove swamps,
sandy beaches, and dense rainforests.

Farming and fishing

Farming is the most important part of Liberia's economy. In some areas, the soil is fertile. The country's many rivers provide good **irrigation**.

Most people in Liberia are **subsistence farmers**. This means that they just grow enough crops to feed their families. The major food crop is rice. Vegetables, **cassava**, **plantain**, and sugarcane are also grown. Fruit trees provide mangoes, bananas, and coconuts. Chickens, goats, and sheep are reared for eggs, milk, and meat.

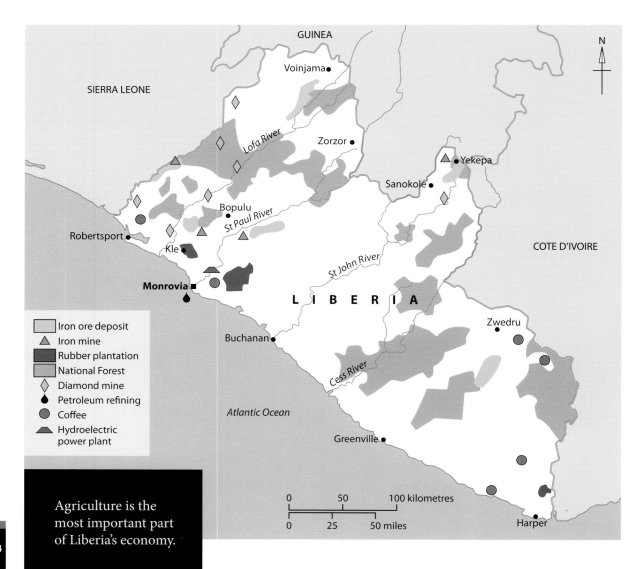

Agriculture is the most important part of Liberia's economy.

Mining for diamonds is a tough job.

Rubber, coffee, and **cacao** are grown on big **plantations**. These goods are then **exported** to other countries. Other cash crops include peanuts, kola nuts, and cotton.

Fish is another important natural resource. The waters off Liberia's Atlantic coast are full of mackerel, barracuda, and red snapper. Some types of fish are also reared in inland ponds.

Mining and timber

A number of different minerals are buried deep within Liberia's soil. The most important for the country is iron ore. Since fighting ended in Liberia, international companies have invested billions of dollars and other currencies to **mine** iron ore from the earth. Gold and diamonds are also mined here.

Timber is another key natural resource. In the past, the government allowed companies to cut down thousands of hectares of trees in tropical forests. The **hardwood** taken from these forests was shipped around the world.

During Liberia's second **civil war**, the **United Nations** placed **embargoes** on Liberian timber and diamonds. This meant that member nations could not buy these materials from Liberia. The embargoes were finally lifted in 2007.

Fixing Liberia's economy

Years of warfare and **corrupt** government destroyed Liberia's economy. Many businesses shut down, and international firms moved out of the country. Crops, roads, and buildings were destroyed. Mines and plantations were shut down. Hundreds of thousands of people fled to nearby countries for safety.

Although conditions improved slightly after the war ended, Liberia remains one of the world's poorest nations. World organizations estimate that as many as eight out of every 10 Liberians live in conditions of extreme **poverty**. **Life expectancy** in Liberia is 60 years, compared to 80 in the UK and 78 in the United States. The number of **unemployed** people in the nation remains high.

Government efforts

Beginning in 2003, Liberia's government took steps to strengthen the economy. Sirleaf and other officials are working to end the corruption. Such corruption has made doing business in Liberia difficult. Liberian leaders have also asked for aid from other countries to rebuild roads and buildings.

Over the past few years, a number of international companies have returned to Liberia. Many are mining companies. They pay the government for the right to dig iron, gold, and diamonds out of Liberia's soil. Oil companies are also exploring the possibility of drilling off the country's coast.

Liberia continues to receive income from its **maritime registry programme**. This programme allows international shipping companies to register their large ships in Liberia, where taxes are low.

Farming remains an important
part of Liberia's economy.
This woman is harvesting rice.

Wildlife: biodiversity in Liberia

Liberia is home to a wide variety of wildlife. The country's forests shelter chimpanzees, several different types of monkeys, pygmy hippopotamuses, and anteaters. Lions, elephants, and leopards roam the countryside.

Many reptiles can be found in Liberia, including crocodiles, lizards, and snakes. Boa constrictors make their homes in the trees. The country has eight different species of poisonous snakes, including black cobras and vipers. Creepy, crawly creatures include scorpions, spiders, and thousands of insect species.

There are nearly 600 different types of birds in Liberia, including parrots, hawks, eagles, and flamingos. Even the waters off Liberia's coast are home to abundant animal life. Many types of fish live there, and whales migrate through the region seasonally.

The pygmy hippo, also known as the Liberian hippo, is a rare species. There may be as few as 2,000 of these animals left in the wild.

When the tree pangolin is frightened, it rolls up in a ball.

War takes a toll

The **civil wars** seriously affected wildlife populations in the nation. During the wars, people hunted wild animals to feed themselves and their families. Some of the creatures were already **endangered** before the war. During the violent times, their numbers dropped close to **extinction**. Such animals include elephants, leopards, and short-horned buffalo. One species of monkey may have become totally extinct. Today, the **United Nations** estimates that 121 species in Liberia are threatened.

Liberian officials realize that the nation's great diversity of wildlife could be used to promote **ecotourism** in their country. They are working hard to ensure that the land – and the creatures living on it – are protected.

Sapo National Park

Sapo National Park, founded in 1983, is Liberia's only national park. The park contains plants and animals that are not found anywhere else in the country. Mining, logging, and hunting are not permitted in the park, and people cannot live there.

Located in a remote area of south-central Liberia, Sapo is not easy to get to. From Monrovia, visitors must travel over rough dirt roads for 10 hours. During the rainy season it is impossible to get to the park.

Like most other parts of Liberia, the park was damaged during the civil wars. Fighting destroyed the park's buildings and other structures. Equipment used to maintain the park was stolen or destroyed. Three park rangers were killed. People also moved into the park, seeking protection in the dense forest.

Protecting the rainforest

Today, the Liberian government is working to bring Sapo National Park back to its former condition. In 2003 officials made the park larger, bringing its size up to 1,800 square kilometres (700 square miles) – slightly larger than the area of London.

Wildlife organizations are also focused on preserving Sapo. The Society for the Conservation of Nature of Liberia (SCNLIB) is the country's oldest wildlife protection group. Group members teach Liberian citizens about how important it is to safeguard the country's land and wildlife.

Sapo National Park was founded in 1983 to preserve one of the few remaining rainforests in Western Africa.

Infrastructure: life in Liberia

Liberia has a population of 4.1 million people. About 97 percent are **indigenous**, or one of the 25 original ethnic groups in Liberia. The rest are either descended from the **Americo-Liberians** or have migrated to Liberia from other countries.

English is the official language in Liberia, but the indigenous peoples of Liberia also speak their own languages. The three major indigenous language groups are Kwa, Mande, and Mel. In all, more than 24 different languages are spoken throughout the country.

Healthcare in Liberia

People in Liberia are at risk of getting a number of serious illnesses. Infectious diseases include HIV/AIDS, hepatitis, typhoid, malaria, and yellow fever. Only a small percentage of Liberians receive the immunization drugs they need to protect them from these diseases.

After the **civil wars**, foreign aid groups helped rebuild some of Liberia's health system. But many people in the nation cannot afford to pay the fees for healthcare. Today, Liberia's government is working to make healthcare accessible for all.

Liberia's government

Liberia's government is modelled on the system in the United States. The government is headed by a president, who is elected by voters for a six-year term. Anyone who is at least 18 years old can vote in elections.

Liberia's lawmaking body is made up of two parts, a Senate and a House of Representatives. The Senate has 30 members; the House has 64. Liberia also has a Supreme Court with five judges.

Conditions in rural areas are very different from those in the city.

Liberia and the world

Since 2006 President Sirleaf and other Liberian officials have worked to improve the way Liberia is viewed around the world. The president has visited many countries. Liberia signed a number of important environmental and economic agreements with other nations.

Liberia, a founding member of the **United Nations**, belongs to several international organizations. Since 2003, UN peacekeeping troops in the country have made sure that warfare does not erupt again. They help to train police and soldiers, and support human rights activities in the nation. Liberia is also a member of the Economic Community of West African States (ECOWAS). This group works to maintain peace and growth in West Africa.

Liberia trades with many countries. Among its top trading partners are South Korea, Germany, Singapore, Poland, and Japan. Materials **imported** into the country include fuel, machinery, and foods.

About 15,000 UN peacekeepers remain in Liberia to make sure that violence does not erupt again.

As president, Ellen Johnson Sirleaf has worked hard to help Liberia recover from the civil wars.

Refugees in other countries

Hundreds of thousands of Liberians still live in other countries. Most live in nearby West African nations. These Liberians live in **refugee** camps in poor conditions. They often endure **discrimination** in the places they live. When they try to return home, they are victims of armed robbers who take what little they have. Today more than 450,000 Liberians have moved to the United States.

Rebuilding education

The long years of civil warfare left Liberia's educational system in tatters. School buildings were destroyed. Teachers were killed or fled the country. Many children were caught up in the fighting. Education in Liberia broke down completely, and **literacy** (the ability to read and write) plummeted. Currently, Liberia has one of the lowest literacy rates in the world.

One of President Sirleaf's top priorities is to revive Liberia's education system. The country's Ministry of Education has worked with groups around the world to rebuild destroyed schools. Groups such as the Liberian Education Trust Fund are training Liberians to be teachers. They also offer **scholarships** to students who want to return to school.

As things settle down, more children return to school. Younger children receive free schooling from kindergarten through to Year 13. In school, they learn English, reading, maths, and other subjects.

Older children are also returning to school. Many must repeat earlier grades that they missed during the war. Former child soldiers are being taught life skills to help them fit back in with their fellow Liberians.

In 2008 nearly seven out of ten school-aged children attended school. Liberians are working to increase this ratio to ten out of ten.

Culture: the heart of Liberia

Monrovia is Liberia's capital and its largest city. Before the wars, there were shops, theatres, and tall buildings. But during the fighting, these businesses were shut down or destroyed. People abandoned their homes and found shelter in **refugee** camps in other countries.

Because of the destruction in Monrovia, few jobs are available in the city. Although things are improving, most people must travel into the country to work on farms. Because very few Liberians own cars, most workers travel everywhere by foot.

Although the **infrastructure** in Monrovia is being rebuilt, conditions remain hard. Many people live without electricity, fresh water, and sewage systems. Phone and Internet access are not usually available, and crime is common.

A few railway lines run from Liberia's interior to the coast. The trains carry goods from **plantations** and **mines** to Monrovia's port for **export**. Liberia also has two main airports.

Life outside Monrovia

Life outside the capital is very different. People in the country live in small villages. Their homes are usually mud huts with **thatched** roofs. As in the cities, there is usually no access to electricity, indoor plumbing, or fresh water. During the dry season, people in some areas must walk for miles to find drinkable water.

Conditions in many villages are not healthy. About one out of every three Liberians is **malnourished**, and healthcare is difficult to obtain.

Monrovia is Liberia's largest and busiest city.

Religion in Liberia

When freed American slaves settled in Liberia in the 1800s, they brought Christianity with them. Today, two out of every five Liberians are Christians. About 12 percent are **Muslims**, and the rest practise the traditional religious beliefs of their **tribe** or ethnic group.

But even those who practise Christianity may also practise the traditional native customs. For example, some Christians also practise juju. Juju is the traditional use of **rituals** and herbs for healing and other purposes.

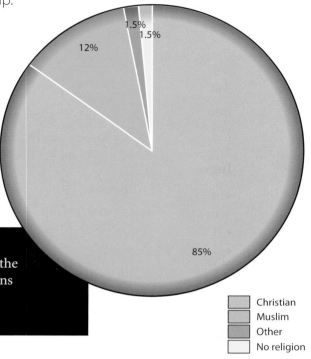

12%

1.5%
1.5%

85%

Christian
Muslim
Other
No religion

This chart shows the division of religions in Liberia.

Liberian women perform a rain dance in their village.

Food

Rice is the main food in Liberia. People eat rice for every meal. On the side are sauces, vegetables, fruits, meats, and fish. The biggest meal of the day is usually the midday meal. Throughout the rest of the day, Liberians might snack on fruit or sugarcane.

Jollof Rice

Jollof rice is a popular dish in Liberia. Ask an adult to help you make it.

Ingredients

- 450 g cooked meat (chicken, bacon, prawns, or smoked pork), cut into 2 cm chunks
- 120 ml of vegetable oil
- 1 onion, finely chopped
- 1 green pepper, finely chopped
- 475 ml tin of whole tomatoes
- 3 tablespoons tomato puree
- ½ tablespoon salt
- ¼ teaspoon black pepper
- ¼ teaspoon thyme
- ½ teaspoon chilli powder
- 340 g cooked, hot rice

Method

1. Cook meat in half the oil until slightly browned.
2. Fry vegetables in a separate pan until soft.
3. Add tomatoes and simmer for 5 minutes.
4. Add tomato puree, 1.5 litres of water, and spices. Stir.
5. Add cooked meat and simmer for 20 more minutes.
6. Place rice in a deep bowl, with meat sauce in the centre. Serve.

Arts and crafts

Liberia is famous for its arts and crafts. Liberians are known for being skilled mask carvers. The masks are used in private rituals and public festivals.

Liberians are also famous for their work with **textiles**. Liberians are so proud of their quilts that they are sometimes presented as gifts to leaders of countries from around the world.

Murals (artwork painted on the walls of buildings) are also popular in Liberia. These often tell a story or celebrate an event in Liberian history. Pottery and weaving are also common in Liberia.

Liberia's carved masks are famous throughout Africa and the world.

Song and dance

Music and dancing are important to all Liberians. The people use song and dance to celebrate at festivals, rituals, weddings, holidays, and other occasions. Music is even heard at funerals.

Liberians use a number of handcrafted instruments to make music. Drums are most important. Some drums are beaten with the hand or a stick. Others are squeezed to make noise. Rattles made from **gourds** are also used.

Famous Liberians

Football is the favourite sport of most Liberians. Liberia's best-known footballer is George Weah. He played for European clubs during his career.

Perhaps the most famous Liberian is William Tubman (1895-1971). Tubman was a descendant of freed slaves who founded the country. From 1944 to his death, he served as Liberia's president. He is sometimes called the founder of modern Liberia because he encouraged tribal groups to take part in running the government.

George Weah is a famous Liberian footballer.

Liberia today

For years, Liberians suffered during a long drawn out **civil war** that devastated their country and people. The country's **infrastructure** and economy – and all other parts of daily life – were completely disrupted. Every part of Liberia was affected by the violence. Normal life was destroyed.

Repairing the damage done during the civil wars has not been easy. Liberia is slowly rebuilding roads, businesses, schools, and hospitals. People are receiving job training, and children are going back to school. Former soldiers are giving up their weapons and resuming normal lives.

Democratic elections are being held on a regular basis. These elections allow Liberians to choose the people who will lead them into the 21st century. In 2008 Liberia even took its first **census**, counting the population for the first time since before the war.

President Sirleaf and the Liberian leaders who come after her face some huge challenges. **Poverty** and illiteracy are just two of the obstacles faced by the country today. The key to Liberia's future is for all Liberians to remain united for change, progress, and peace. If that happens, then the future looks bright for the people of Liberia.

Young people who lost limbs during the civil wars still have the will and skills needed to compete and win.

A bucket collects rubber from a tree on a **plantation** in Liberia.

Fact file

Official name: Republic of Liberia

Languages: English (official); more than 24 other native African languages spoken

Capital: Monrovia, established: 1822

Type of government: Republic

Monrovia is the seat of Liberia's national government. This photo shows the government buildings.

Current leader: Ellen Johnson Sirleaf, nicknamed the "Iron Lady"

Religions: Christianity, Islam, native African religions

National anthem: "All Hail Liberia, Hail"

All hail, Liberia hail
All hail, Liberia hail
This glorious land of liberty shall long be ours
Though new her name green be her fame
And mighty be her power
In joy and gladness with our hearts united
We'll shout the freedom of a race benighted
A home of glorious liberty by God's command

All hail, Liberia hail
All hail, Liberia hail
In union strong, success is sure
We cannot fail
With God above our rights to prove
We will over all prevail
With hearts and hands, our country's cause defending
We'll meet the foe with valour unpretending

Largest cities: Monrovia (est. population: 1,000,00), Buchanan (est. population 300,000), Ganta (est. population 290,000), Gbarnga (est. population 150,000), Harbel (est. population 136,000), Kakata (est. population 100,000)

Population: 4.1 million (est. 2010); aged 14 and under: 42.7%

Life expectancy: 59 years (men); 61 years (women)

Total land area: 111,369 square kilometres (43,000 square miles)

Seal: Liberia's Great Seal shows a sailing ship, a palm tree, and a plough and axe. The motto on the seal is "The Love of Liberty Brought Us Here."

Currency:	Liberian dollar (L$); the Liberian dollar is worth 62 pence
Average annual income Per person:	£106
Exports:	rubber, iron ore, cacao, coffee, mahogany and other wood, rice, bananas, diamonds
Imports:	fuels, chemicals, machinery, transportation equipment, food

Festivals and holidays:

1 January	New Year's Day
11 February	Armed Forces Day
14 May	Unification Day
26 July	Independence Day
25 December	Christmas

Highest elevation:	Mount Wuteve: 1,380 metres (4,528 feet)
Lowest point:	Atlantic Ocean: 0 metres (0 feet)
Climate:	Average temperature: 27°C (80°F)
	Hottest temperature: 34°C (93°F)
	Coldest temperature: 13°C (55°F)
	Average rainfall per year: 508 cm (200 inches)
Coastline:	579 kilometres (360 miles)
Longest river:	Cavalla River 515 kilometres (320 miles)

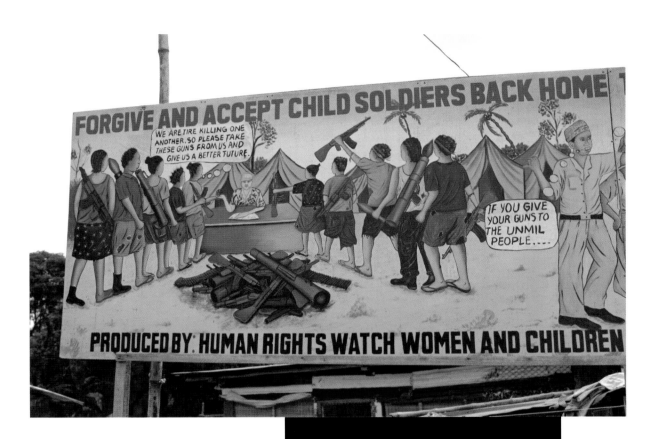

A billboard encourages Liberians to accept former child soldiers back into society after they've turned in their weapons.

Timeline

BC is short for "before Christ". BC is added after a date and means that the date occurred before the birth of Jesus Christ, for example, 450 BC.

AD is short for Anno Domini, which is Latin for "in the year of our Lord". AD is added before a date and means that the date occurred after the birth of Jesus Christ, for example, AD 720.

AD

1100s	The first people, ancestors of the Bassa, Dey, and other **tribes**, settle in what is now Liberia.
Early 1800s	Sixteen different tribes make their homes in Liberia.
1500s-1600s	European explorers claim most of Africa for their countries.
1822	Freed slaves from the United States begin arriving in Liberia.
1847	**Americo-Liberians** form the **Republic** of Liberia, the first republic in Africa's history.
1848	Liberia holds first elections.
1862	The University of Liberia, a public institution, is founded in Monrovia.
1944	William Tubman starts his first term as president of Liberia.
1971	William Tubman dies during his seventh term as president.
1980	A rebellion led by Samuel Doe overthrows the Liberian government.
1983	Sapo National Park is founded.

1985	Ellen Johnson Sirleaf is sentenced to 10 years in prison for speaking out against the Liberian President, Samuel Doe.
1989	Liberia's first **civil war** begins; Charles Taylor takes control of government.
1990	President Doe is executed by **rebel** forces.
1996	Civil war ends.
1997	Charles Taylor is elected as Liberia's president.
1999	Liberia's second civil war begins.
2002	About 230,000 Liberians flee the country to escape violence.
2003	Thousands of women form the Women of Liberia Mass Action for Peace movement.
August 2003	Peace negotiations result in an end to the second civil war.
October 2003	Sapo National Park is expanded.
2005	Sirleaf defeats famous footballer George Weah to become Liberia's – and Africa's – first female president.
2008	Liberia conducts its first post-war **census**.
2010	Sirleaf is re-elected as Liberia's president.

Glossary

abolitionist person who works for the end of slavery

Americo-Liberians people in Liberia descended from freed US slaves who founded the country in 1822

cacao seed used to make chocolate and cocoa

cassava starchy plant found in the tropics

census official count of the people in a country

civil war extended conflict, usually violent, between two or more groups within a country

colonize form a colony or colonies in

colony settlement controlled by a distant foreign power

convert convince someone to give up their old religion for a new one

corrupt dishonest, bad

discrimination unfair or unjust treatment of people

economics study of how a society creates, uses, and distributes goods

ecotourism tourism that centres around an area's natural habitats

embargo order preventing goods from being shipped into or out of a country

endangered in danger of dying out

equator imaginary line around the middle of Earth

export ship goods out of a country for sale in another country

extinction act of completely wiping out a species

fertile (regarding land) capable of abundant plant growth **gourd** squash-like fruit with a hard outer skin

hardwood hard, compact wood from trees, used to build furniture and other items

humid moist, damp

import ship goods into a country from other nations

indigenous native to an area

infrastructure structures such as roads, buildings, and sewers, that are necessary for a healthy society

irrigation water supplied to land for growing

life expectancy total number of years that a person can expect to live

literacy ability to read and write

malnourished not having enough to eat and stay healthy

maritime registry programme process through which ship owners in other lands register their ships in Liberia because of lower taxes and fewer regulations

mine remove metals, rocks, or minerals from the ground

Muslim follower of Islam, a religion based on the Koran and the teachings of the prophet Muhammad

negotiate work out terms of an agreement

non-violent protest rallies, parades, and sit-ins that involve no violent actions

peace treaty agreement signed by two or more parties that ends warfare

plantain large, starchy banana found in the tropics

plantation large farm, often in tropical areas

poverty condition of being poor

rebel someone who fights against authority

refugee person who lives away from home in order to remain safe

republic country or state where the citizens elect representatives to serve in the government

ritual regularly followed routine

scholarship money or other aid that allows a student to continue his or her studies

subsistence farmer farmer who grows just enough food to feed him or herself and his or her own family

textiles woven fabrics, cloth

thatched covered with straw or leaves

tribe group of people sharing the same ancestors, customs, and beliefs

unemployed without a job or paid work

United Nations (UN) worldwide organization that promotes world peace and social justice

Find out more

Books

Africa (Facts At Your Fingertips), Derek Hall (Wayland, 2008)

Liberia: A Question and Answer Book, Muriel L. Dubois (Capstone, 2005)

Countries of the World: Liberia, Patricia Levy and Michael Spilling (Marshall Cavendish Benchmark, 2009)

Africa and the Slave Trade (Black History), Dan Lyndon (Franklin Watts, 2010)

Encyclopedia of World Geography, Jane Bingham, et al. (Eds), (Usborne, 2010)

Websites

www.ecowas.int
This is the home page of the Economic Community of West African States, with information on each member state and recent decisions.

www.emansion.gov.lr
This is the home page of the governor's mansion in Liberia, with information on President Sirleaf and current events happening in the country.

www.liberia-un.org
This is Liberia's United Nations page.

http://liberiapastandpresent.org
This website has information on all things Liberian. It was created by a Dutch professor who works for the Ministry of Foreign Affairs in the Netherlands.

Places to visit

Sapo National Park
Sinoe County, Liberia
Liberia's only national park protects natural rainforest habitat.

Further research

After reading the book, what do you find most interesting about Liberia?
What might be some other challenges the country faces?
To learn more, you might want to research the following topics:
- William Tubman, Samuel Doe, Charles Taylor, or Ellen Johnson Sirleaf
- Liberia's Maritime Registry Programme
- American Colonization Society
- Women of Liberia Mass Action for Peace
- Sapo National Park
- West Africa's tropical rainforests

You can visit your local library to learn more about any of these fascinating subjects.

Topic tools

You can use these topic tools for your school projects. Trace the map on to a sheet of paper, using the thick black outline to guide you.

Liberia's flag, adopted in 1847, is based on the flag of the United States. The flag features 11 equal horizontal stripes of red (six) and white (five). Each stripe represents one of the 11 original signers of Liberia's Declaration of Independence. A white five-pointed star appears on a blue square in the upper left corner. The blue square represents Africa, and the white star represents the freedom granted to the ex-slaves who founded the nation. According to Liberia's constitution, the blue colour represents liberty, justice, and fidelity. The white colour represents purity and cleanliness, and the red denotes steadfastness, valour, and fervour.

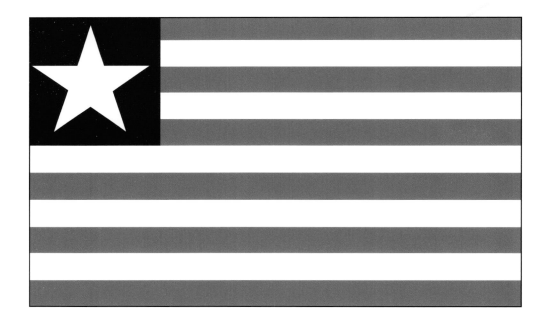

N

■ **Monrovia**

Index

Titles in the series

Afghanistan	978 1 406 22778 9	Japan	978 1 406 23548 7
Algeria	978 1 406 23561 6	Latvia	978 1 406 22795 6
Australia	978 1 406 23533 3	Liberia	978 1 406 23563 0
Brazil	978 1 406 22785 7	Libya	978 1 406 23564 7
Canada	978 1 406 23534 0	Lithuania	978 1 406 22796 3
Chile	978 1 406 22786 4	Mexico	978 1 406 22790 1
China	978 1 406 23547 0	Morocco	978 1 406 23565 4
Costa Rica	978 1 406 22787 1	New Zealand	978 1 406 23536 4
Cuba	978 1 406 22788 8	North Korea	978 1 406 23549 4
Czech Republic	978 1 406 22792 5	Pakistan	978 1 406 22782 6
Egypt	978 1 406 23562 3	Philippines	978 1 406 23550 0
England	978 1 406 22799 4	Poland	978 1 406 22797 0
Estonia	978 1 406 22793 2	Portugal	978 1 406 23578 4
France	978 1 406 22800 7	Russia	978 1 406 23579 1
Germany	978 1 406 22801 4	Scotland	978 1 406 22803 8
Greece	978 1 406 23575 3	South Africa	978 1 406 23537 1
Haiti	978 1 406 22789 5	South Korea	978 1 406 23551 7
Hungary	978 1 406 22794 9	Spain	978 1 406 23580 7
Iceland	978 1 406 23576 0	Tunisia	978 1 406 23566 1
India	978 1 406 22779 6	United States of America	978 1 406 23538 8
Iran	978 1 406 22780 2	Vietnam	978 1 406 23552 4
Iraq	978 1 406 22781 9	Wales	978 1 406 22804 5
Ireland	978 1 406 23577 7	Yemen	978 1 406 22783 3
Israel	978 1 406 23535 7		
Italy	978 1 406 22802 1		